T0014553

What's in a name? You have one. It is important for you. Your name has meaning.

Bible names often help us understand key aspects of the individual and their life.

This fascinating resource on names in the Bible teaches us many lessons but most of all draws us to the best name of all – the Lord Jesus Christ.

Carine Mackenzie
Author of the Bible Wise series and
Psalms for my Day

10 9 8 7 6 5 4 3 2 1

Copyright © 2022 Jean Stapleton

ISBN: 978-1-5271-0917-9

Published by Christian Focus Publications,
Geanies House, Fearn, Tain, Ross-shire,
IV20 1TW, Scotland, U.K.
www.christianfocus.com;
email: info@christianfocus.com

Designed and typeset by Pete Barnsley (CreativeHoot.com)

Printed and bound by Imago, Turkey

WHO is WHO?

40 BIBLE NAMES & THEIR MEANING

JEAN STAPLETON

CF4·K

CONTENTS

5

INTRODUCTION

Parents give lots of thought to what name to give to their new baby. Do you know why your name was chosen? You may be called after someone in your family, such as one of your grandparents. You may have been given a name with a meaning that your parents liked. For example, the popular boys' name John, means 'God is merciful', while the girls' name Margaret, means 'pearl'.

Many Bible names have meanings that fit the person's life, or a message connected to the time they lived in. Some names were given by God even before the baby was born, such as Abraham and Sarah's son Isaac and Zacharias and Elizabeth's son John.

In this book you will read about some well-known Bible characters, and others you may never have heard of.

A book about names could not leave out the most wonderful names of all: what the names given to the Lord Jesus mean, especially to those who trust in Him.

JEAN STAPLETON

1 ADAM, THE FIRST MAN
Genesis 1:27

The first chapter of Genesis tells us about God's creation: the earth, sun, moon and stars; the plants, fish, birds and animals. However, there was something very special about the creation of man: he was to be made 'in the image of God'. It is not easy to explain exactly what this means, but we know that men and women have understanding, can think and feel, appreciate beauty and most important of all, can know and love God. It is not correct to say that man is an animal who has somehow become more successful than other animals. God made mankind to take charge of the earth, which includes all the plants and animals (Genesis 1:28).

The name Adam means 'man', or 'mankind'. We are told that God formed Adam and breathed life into him. God prepared Adam's home: a beautiful garden with a great variety of fruit trees, which Adam was free to eat from as he wished. Two trees in the garden had particular names: the tree of life and the tree of the knowledge of good and evil.

God gave Adam just one rule, so that by his obedience, he could show his love and trust for the God who had given him so much. God told Adam that there was just one tree from which he must not eat: the tree of knowledge of good and evil. Adam was warned that disobedience would bring death, because he would be separated from God, who is the source of life.

Genesis chapter three gives us the sad account of how Adam disobeyed God, bringing sin, suffering and death into the world. Adam's perfect body began to show the changes that would lead to his death. His life of fellowship with God ended, when he disobeyed his loving Creator.

BiBLE SEARCH:
Genesis chapter 1; Genesis 2:7-9; 15-17.

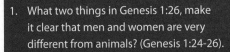

1. What two things in Genesis 1:26, make it clear that men and women are very different from animals? (Genesis 1:24-26).

2. What was the one rule that God gave to Adam? (Genesis 2:16-17).

3. What would be the result of disobedience? (Genesis 2:17).

2 EVE, THE FIRST BRIDE
Genesis 3:20

All that God created was perfect. God Himself saw that everything He had made was 'very good' (Genesis 1:31). Adam was a perfect man, and yet God said that there was one thing that was not good (Read Genesis 2:18).

Before God carried out His promise to make a suitable helper for Adam, He brought animals to Adam, for him to give them names. As he did this, Adam realised that no animal was a suitable companion for him. You can't really have a conversation with your pet or discuss things that puzzle you, can you?

God caused Adam to go into a deep sleep; and He then took a part of Adam's side and from this He formed the first woman. We might wonder why God formed the first woman in this way. However, the Bible makes it clear, that the way Eve was created shows the close relationship of husband and wife. When the Lord Jesus was asked a question about marriage, He answered with the words of Genesis 2:24 (Matthew 19:5).

We do not know how long the perfect happiness that Adam and Eve enjoyed lasted. Sadly, a day came when everything changed. The devil deceived Eve: he persuaded her that God was withholding something good from her. Instead of remembering that God had given her life and everything she needed, Eve broke the one rule that God had given. She took fruit from the tree of the knowledge of good and evil and shared it with Adam.

Instead of loving obedience to God, Adam and Eve acted in sinful disobedience. We read about the consequences of this for Adam and Eve in Genesis chapter 3. These consequences can still be seen today in wars and conflicts, suffering and death.

Adam understood that from Eve's children, the population would grow. He gave her the name Eve which means 'life' or 'living'.

BiBLE SEARCH:

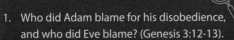

Genesis 2:15-25; Genesis chapter 3.

1. Who did Adam blame for his disobedience, and who did Eve blame? (Genesis 3:12-13).

2. Does the New Testament confirm that the early chapters of Genesis are absolutely true? Explain your answer from 1 Corinthians 15:21-22.

3. Genesis 3:15 is the first promise of a Saviour. Who was it who bruised (or crushed) the serpent's head?

13

3 THE LONGEST LIFE
Genesis 5:27

The Bible tells us that before the flood of Noah's time, people lived very long lives. Genesis chapter five gives us a list of Adam's descendants, and Methuselah is the seventh on the list after Adam. His father's name was Enoch and the New Testament tells us that Enoch was a prophet (Jude 14-15). Enoch may have understood that God's punishment was going to come because of mankind's wickedness. This may be the reason for the name given to his son, which many people believe means, 'when he dies, it shall be sent.' It certainly is the case that it was in the year that Methuselah died, that God sent the great flood. (This can be worked out from the ages given in Genesis chapter 5.)

The message that runs throughout the Old Testament, is that God is going to send a Saviour into the world. The list of names in Genesis chapter five can be found, in reverse order, in Luke 3:36-38. This chapter traces the genealogy (family tree) of Jesus all the way back to Adam, the first man.

We learn more details of the coming of the Saviour as we read further into the Old Testament. The Saviour was to be born through Abraham's descendants: the nation of Israel. Within that nation, He would come from the family of King David. You might ask why this is the great theme of the Bible. From the time of Adam, sin has cut us off from a perfectly pure and holy God, who is the source of life. We could not put this right. Other world religions say we must do something to satisfy the god we worship. Only the Bible tells us what God has done. He has sent His Son, the Lord Jesus, to take the punishment for the sin of everyone who trusts in Him. He also lived a sinless life of perfect obedience to His Father, on behalf of His people who could not do this.

BiBLE SEARCH:

**Genesis 5:21-27; Luke 3:36-38;
Isaiah 9:6-7.**

1. What happened in the year that Methuselah died?

2. What relation was Methuselah to Noah? (Genesis 5:25-29).

3. Why are the names listed in Genesis 5 repeated in Luke 3?

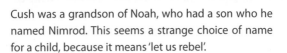

4 THE REBEL
Genesis 10:8

Cush was a grandson of Noah, who had a son who he named Nimrod. This seems a strange choice of name for a child, because it means 'let us rebel'.

There are just a few verses in Genesis about Nimrod (Genesis 10:8-12). After the flood, Nimrod became a great leader who founded several cities. One of those cities was Babel.

The building of the city and tower of Babel, was an act of rebellion against God. God had instructed Noah and his sons to fill the earth. It was His purpose that mankind should have control of God's creation throughout the world. This meant, not being tyrants, but taking care of God's creation.

The builders of Babel were in defiance of what God had said. They wanted to become a powerful people by not being scattered to different places. Nimrod must have been the leader in this rebellion. He found that it is impossible to stop God from doing what he is going to do.

The building work stopped, when God caused the people to speak different languages. Many could not understand one another, so groups who did speak the same language must have separated. This was the beginning of the different nations who settled in many lands.

All through history there have been men who, like Nimrod, have wanted to be empire-builders. As at Babel, God sometimes brings down the powerful, such as the fall of Babylon that we read about in the Book of Daniel (Daniel 5:30).

Christians in many countries still suffer persecution. We look forward to the day when the Lord Jesus will come again, and all those who love Him will be with Him for ever. That will be a time of great joy: no more sorrow, suffering or death. No more rebellion against our wonderful Creator.

BiBLE SEARCH:

Genesis 10:8-12; Genesis 11:1-9; Revelation 21:1-5.

1. In what way did the Babel-builders rebel against God? (Genesis 9:1; Genesis 11:4).

2. How was the building stopped? (Genesis 11:7).

3. What four things will no longer happen, when God makes everything new? (Revelation 21:4).

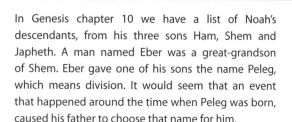

5 PELEG
Genesis 10:25

In Genesis chapter 10 we have a list of Noah's descendants, from his three sons Ham, Shem and Japheth. A man named Eber was a great-grandson of Shem. Eber gave one of his sons the name Peleg, which means division. It would seem that an event that happened around the time when Peleg was born, caused his father to choose that name for him.

There are two other verses in Genesis chapter 10 that tell us more about the division that took place (Genesis 10:5 and 32). These verses make it clear that it was the different languages that caused the division of Peleg's time. Before the great flood, everyone had spoken the same language. It is hard for us to imagine the confusion, when people suddenly found that they could not understand one another.

Over the centuries, these different people groups developed their own way of life. We call this the national 'culture', and you will notice differences of culture, when you stay in other countries. Nations also developed different religions. God has given us an understanding that there must be someone greater than ourselves.

However, when people reject the true God, they invent false gods. Man-made religion is all about what we must do to please the god we worship. This may include pilgrimages, fastings or doing penance for our sins. Only the God of the Bible sent His Son to be our Saviour, because we can never satisfy His perfect holiness.

Different nationalities may look different, but the Book of Acts reminds us that we are all descendants from the first man and woman that God created (Acts 17:26). We all have the same instruction from God to care for His creation. We should pray that people from all nations will hear the message of the gospel.

BiBLE SEARCH:

Genesis 9:1; Genesis 10:5, 25 and 32;
Genesis 11:1-9; Acts 17:26.

1. What was God's instruction to Adam and Eve, that was repeated to Noah? (Genesis 1:28 and 9:1).

2. What did the Babel-builders want to avoid? (Genesis 11:4).

3. What event was Peleg named after? (Genesis 10:25).

6 ABRAM THEN ABRAHAM

Genesis 17:5

We first read about Abram in Genesis chapter 11, where we are told that he was one of three sons of Terah. Terah and his family lived in the city of Ur, which is in present-day Iraq.

God told Abram to leave Ur, and travel to a country which He would show him. With this command came a promise, that a great nation would come from Abram's family and also that good would come to families throughout the world through him.

Abram left Ur with his wife Sarai, his father Terah and his nephew Lot. They travelled over five hundred miles north to Haran. They remained there until Terah died and then Abram, Sarai and Lot travelled south into the land of Canaan. As they travelled on through Canaan, God spoke to Abram. He said that this was the land that He would give to his descendants.

Abram was seventy-five years old when he left Haran and at that time he had no children. God had already promised that Abram's family would become a great nation. Now God was providing a land for that nation.

It was when Abram was ninety-nine years old that God told him that his name was to be changed to Abraham. The name Abram means 'exalted father', but the name Abraham means 'father of a multitude'. This confirmed God's promise that Abraham would have many descendants.

When Abraham was one hundred years old, he and his wife had their long-awaited son, Isaac. Their faith had been tested, but we read that Abraham believed God (Genesis 15:6). After Abraham's death, Isaac became the head of this family and inherited the promises God had made to his father. Like his parents, Isaac waited many years for any children to be born. Twenty years after Isaac and Rebekah were married, their twin sons were born.

BiBLE SEARCH:

Genesis 12:1-4; Genesis 17:1-8.

1. What promise made to Abraham would affect the entire world? (Genesis 12:3).

2. How was this promise fulfilled? (Matthew 1:1 and 16-17).

7 SARAI BECAME SARAH

Genesis 17:15

We are introduced to Sarai in Genesis chapter 11, where we are told that she was Abram's wife but had no children. We do not know how Sarai felt about leaving her home in Ur. It was a long journey, in days when travelling was not easy. Also, her husband was not able to tell her where they would live in the future, because he did not know (Hebrews 11:8). They were leaving Ur in obedience to God's words.

Sarai would have been used to a comfortable home in Ur, which was an advanced city at that time (about 2000 B.C.). However, in the land of Canaan, Sarai would become a tent-dweller. No doubt her life was very different from what she had known before.

When Sarai was eighty-nine years old, God told Abraham that his wife's name was to be Sarah, which means 'princess'. It is not certain what the name Sarai meant: some people think that it meant 'contention' or 'argument'. God promised to bless Sarah, who He said would become 'a mother of nations'.

Sarah's life would not have been easy, but the birth of a son, Isaac, when she was ninety years old, must have been a great joy to her. Her experience of waiting so long for the birth of a child must have taught her a great deal about faith in God. She learned that God always does what He promises. We may be prevented from keeping a promise by a change in our circumstances. God is always able to do what He has said He will do.

BiBLE SEARCH:

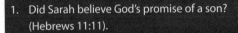

Genesis 17:15-16;
Genesis 18:1 and 10-15; Genesis 21:1-7.

1. Did Sarah believe God's promise of a son? (Hebrews 11:11).

2. Had she always found it easy to believe God's promises? (Genesis 18:10-15).

8 THE HAIRY BABY

Genesis 25:25

Isaac and Rebekah's twin boys were quite different. The first to be born had hairy skin. The name Esau means 'hairy'. Jacob's appearance is not mentioned, but later in his life he described himself as smooth skinned.

As the twins grew up, their characters were also different. Esau liked to be out-of-doors hunting. Jacob showed more understanding of God's promises. Jacob did not marry, until advised by his father to seek a wife from Abraham's relatives at Haran. It was important that Jacob's wife should not be an idol-worshipping Canaanite. Esau had not understood this and had married two Hittite women and this greatly troubled Isaac and Rebekah.

Esau was not concerned when he gave away his birthright in exchange for a meal. But when he realised that Jacob had also received Isaac's blessing, he was distressed. He was also very angry, even threatening to kill his brother. Rebekah knew that Jacob would have to go away for his own safety. She spoke to Isaac about the sorrow she felt about Esau's pagan wives.

Isaac spoke to Jacob. He told him to go to Haran to find a wife from Rebekah's brother Laban's family.

The family in Haran were also relatives of Abraham. Rebekah thought that Jacob would need to be away for a short time. She could not have known that he would stay in Haran for twenty years. We do not know whether Rebekah ever saw Jacob again.

When Jacob returned to Canaan, he still feared his brother's anger. But God heard Jacob's prayer and Esau greeted him kindly. However, Esau's descendants, who became the nation of Edom, were bitter enemies of Jacob's descendants, the nation of Israel.

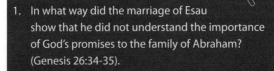

BiBLE SEARCH:

Genesis 25:21-34; Genesis 26:34-35; Genesis 27:46–28:9.

1. In what way did the marriage of Esau show that he did not understand the importance of God's promises to the family of Abraham? (Genesis 26:34-35).

2. How did Rebekah think that Esau would respond to Jacob going away? How long did she expect Jacob to be away? (Genesis 27:44-45).

3. What did Esau observe about Jacob? (Genesis 28:6-7).

9 JACOB THEN ISRAEL

Genesis 32:28

The name Jacob means 'supplanter' or 'deceitful'. In fact Jacob did supplant, or, take the place of, his brother Esau. The brothers were twins, but Esau was born first so it was expected that Esau would become the head of the family, after the death of their father Isaac. This was particularly important in this family, where the head of the family would inherit God's promises to Abraham. However, this family position became Jacob's rather than his 'older' brother's.

At his mother's suggestion, Jacob had deceived his father to make sure that Isaac's blessing was given to Jacob and not to Esau. We do not read in the Bible of blame attached to Jacob for his actions, as it was to Esau for his (Hebrews 12:16-17). He and his mother, Rebekah, were obviously concerned that what God had said should be carried out (Genesis 25:21-23). Jacob was not a child when this took place, and had he and his mother talked and prayed about these matters, Rebekah's plan to deceive Isaac might have been avoided.

After twenty years away from the land of Canaan, Jacob set out with his family to return there. Fearing the anger of his brother Esau, he remained alone to pray through the night, before meeting him. He had a memorable and mysterious experience. It seems that his pleading with God was so intense, that it became a physical struggle. Jacob refused to give up the struggle until he was sure of God's blessing.

It was at this point in his life that Jacob's name was changed. God said that he should now be called Israel, which means 'Prince with God' or, 'one who has prevailed'.

Jacob's prayer was answered and Esau showed no anger as they met. Although his life was far from easy, Jacob did experience God's blessing. From his twelve sons came the twelve tribes of the nation of Israel.

BiBLE SEARCH:

Genesis 25:21-23; Genesis 27;
Genesis 28:1-5.

1. Why was Jacob afraid that Esau would still be angry with him? (Genesis 27:36 and 41-45).

2. What did Jacob do because he was afraid? (Genesis 32:7-12).

3. Were Jacob's fears about Esau realised? (Genesis 33:1-4).

10 BEN-ONI TO BENJAMIN

Genesis 35:18

Rachel was Jacob's first love. She was his cousin, the daughter of his uncle Laban at Haran. As was common at that time, he had more than one wife, but he loved Rachel. During fourteen years in Haran, Jacob's family grew so that he had ten sons and one daughter. However, Rachel had no children, until her son Joseph was born, Jacob's eleventh son. After Joseph's birth, they remained in Haran for six years before returning to Canaan.

Jacob and his family settled in the city of Shechem before living at Bethel. They then set out on another journey when Rachel was expecting her second child. Near to the town of Bethlehem, Rachel's boy was born. However, Rachel was very ill, and because of this she named the little boy Ben-Oni, which means 'son of my sorrow'. Jacob did not allow the child to be called by such a sad name, and so he changed it to Benjamin, which means 'son of the right hand'. Sadly, Rachel died and was buried on the way to Bethlehem. Jacob set up a pillar to mark the grave.

In the New Testament, we find a quotation from Jeremiah the prophet (Jeremiah 31:15): '… Rachel weeping for her children …' (Matthew 2:18). Here, Rachel becomes a picture of the sorrow of the people of Bethlehem, after King Herod destroyed the young children there. This evil deed was done because Herod thought he could destroy the Lord Jesus, who had been born in Bethlehem. However, God had warned Joseph of Herod's intention and in obedience to what God had told him, Joseph had taken Mary and the Child Jesus into Egypt, where they were safe from harm.

BIBLE SEARCH:

Genesis 29:1-20; Matthew 2:1-18.

1. Where did Jacob and Rachel meet? (Genesis 29:2 and 9-10).

2. Why did seven years in Haran pass quickly for Jacob? (Genesis 29:18-20).

3. Why did King Herod have all the little boys up to two years old, in Bethlehem killed? (Matthew 2:1-18).

4. What is used to picture the sadness of parents in Bethlehem? (Matthew 2:18).

11 RENAMED IN EGYPT

Genesis 41:45

Joseph was the eleventh son of Jacob. He was hated by his elder brothers because they believed he was their father's favourite. They sold him as a slave to be taken to the land of Egypt. There he was trusted by his master who put him in charge of his household. However, his master's wife told lies about Joseph and he was unjustly imprisoned.

Even in prison, Joseph was found to be so trustworthy, that he was put in charge of other prisoners. God enabled him to interpret the dreams of two troubled prisoners. One of those prisoners, Pharaoh's chief butler, was released two years later. When Pharaoh was troubled by dreams, his butler remembered Joseph. When he told Pharaoh about him, Joseph was immediately sent for and brought from the prison. Again, God helped Joseph, so that he was able to tell Pharaoh that his dreams meant that after seven years of good harvests, Egypt would have seven years of famine.

Joseph did more than this. He also told Pharaoh that he should put a wise man in charge of the harvests during the good years. Officials should then be appointed to collect grain and store it, so that there would be a reserve for the years of famine that would come.

The result of this advice was that Pharaoh appointed Joseph to take on this task. In fact, Joseph would become the second most important man in the land, after the Pharaoh. At the time of his promotion to high office, Pharaoh gave Joseph the name Zaphnath-Paaneah.

The name Joseph means 'He will add' as his mother Rachel believed that God would give her another son. The name Zaphnath-Paaneah probably means 'God speaks and He lives'. We do not find this new name used again in the Bible account of Joseph's life.

BiBLE SEARCH:

Genesis 41.

1. What advice did Joseph give to Pharaoh? (Genesis 41:33-36).

2. Why did Pharaoh promote Joseph? (Genesis 41:37-40).

12 NAMED BY A PRINCESS
Exodus 2:10

Moses was born at a very dangerous time for baby boys. Pharaoh, the ruler of Egypt, had ordered the killing of all boys born into Israelite families. He was not happy about so many Israelites living in his land. He feared that they would join with Egypt's enemies to defeat his people. He had forgotten that it had been an Israelite, Joseph, who had saved Egypt during seven years of famine. The Pharaoh at that time had been glad to have Joseph's family move into Egypt.

Life became very difficult for Israelite families. Apart from the killing of little boys, there was also forced labour, making bricks and building cities for the Egyptians. However, Amram and Jochebed, Moses' parents, made every effort to save their little one. Jochebed took a basket made of bulrushes and made it waterproof. She placed the baby in the basket and laid it in the reeds by the river bank. Moses' sister Miriam stayed nearby to see what would happen.

The baby was found by Pharaoh's daughter, who felt sorry for the little one. Miriam asked whether she could bring one of the Israelite women to look after him. This was agreed and so, of course, Miriam brought her mother. The princess said that she would pay Jochebed to look after the child. So this baby boy was protected and cared for.

When the child was old enough, Jochebed took him to the princess, who accepted him as her son. She named him Moses, which means 'drawn out', because she had drawn him out of the water. Even though Moses would have had many privileges as the son of Pharaoh's daughter, he never forgot that the Israelites were his people. One day he would learn that he was the man who God had chosen to lead the Israelites out of their slavery in Egypt.

BiBLE SEARCH:

Exodus 1 to 2:10; Hebrews 11:23.

1. Why did Amram and Jochebed act as they did? (Hebrews 11:23).

2. Why did Pharaoh's daughter save Moses? (Exodus 2:6).

13 DISTINGUISHED
Exodus 3:1

The name Jethro probably means 'excellence', or 'distinguished'. We read about Jethro in the book of Exodus, and find that he had some excellent qualities.

Moses had left Egypt when he was forty years old and had settled in the land of Midian. There he married Zipporah, one of Jethro's daughters. Moses became a shepherd to Jethro's flocks and it was while he was looking after the flock, that God spoke to him. Moses saw a bush that appeared to be on fire, but was not being burnt away. As he went to take a closer look, God called him by name, and told him that he must return to Egypt and speak to the Pharaoh. God knew all about the suffering of the Israelites in Egypt and He told Moses that he would bring them out of Egypt. Moses told God why he could not carry out such a task. God told Moses why he should.

Moses did return to Egypt, taking his wife and his two sons with him. We read about the ten plagues that God sent, before Pharaoh finally said that the Israelites must go (Exodus chapters 7–12). Zipporah went with her two sons, back to Jethro's home but they returned to Moses, with Jethro in Exodus chapter 18. When Moses told Jethro all that God had done to help the Israelites since they left Egypt, Jethro was glad. Although he came from Midian where idols were worshipped, he now knew that the God of Israel was the truly great God.

It was at this time that we see Jethro giving excellent advice to his son-in-law. Jethro observed how Moses spent the whole day, hearing from the people about their difficulties. Moses explained God's law to the people and also settled any disputes that arose between them. Jethro realised that Moses would become exhausted. He advised Moses to select able men to judge the people in small matters. They would still bring the larger cases to Moses and Moses would still teach the people how to apply God's law to their situations. Moses followed this good advice.

BiBLE SEARCH:

Exodus 3:1-12; Exodus 18.

1. What three things did Moses tell Jethro? (Exodus 18:8).

2. What did Jethro observe? (Exodus 18:13-14).

3. What was Jethro's advice? (Exodus 18:19-22).

4. What had Jethro learned? (Exodus 18:11).

14 ACHAN THE TROUBLER

Joshua 7:25

God had given the Israelites a great victory at Jericho. They thought that the next city, Ai, would be quite easy to overcome. How wrong they were: they were completely defeated. Joshua, the leader of the Israelites, was very distressed. He called upon God, asking Him why He had allowed His people to have such a defeat. God made it clear to Joshua that someone had sinned. The people had been instructed that they must not take anything from Jericho for themselves. Someone had disobeyed.

Joshua did exactly as God told him to do. Early the next day, he called for the various tribes to come before him. God told Joshua that the tribe of Judah must be gone through, family by family. Then the family of Zabdi had to be looked at one by one. Zabdi's grandson, Achan, was found to be guilty.

When Joshua spoke to Achan, he admitted that he had sinned. He had disobeyed God's instructions, and taken some clothing, silver and gold from Jericho. Joshua sent men to Achan's tent and they found the things hidden there. Achan's sin was very serious because he had deliberately disobeyed God, and so he was put to death.

The place where all this happened was named The Valley of Achor, which means, 'The Valley of Trouble'. Once this sin had been dealt with, God helped the Israelites to once again have victory.

The Valley of Achor is mentioned by the prophet Hosea, when he calls it 'a door of hope'. It may sound strange to speak of trouble that leads to hope, not sorrow. However, it points us to a place of great trouble, where the Son of God was crucified and which is for the Christian, their own place of hope. It is the place where the Lord Jesus took the punishment for the sin of all who trust in Him, giving them the certain hope of being with Him for ever.

BiBLE SEARCH:

Joshua 7; Hosea 2:15.

1. What was the instruction that Achan disobeyed? (Joshua 6:17-19 and Deuteronomy 7:25-26).

2. What four things do we read about Achan in Joshua 7:21?

15 NEW NAME FOR GIDEON

Judges 6:32

Gideon lived in difficult days in Israel. The people had disobeyed God by worshipping the idols of the nations around them: Gideon's father actually had an altar and an image of Baal. Because of their idolatry, God allowed the enemies of Israel to trouble them. The Midianites and the Amalekites came in great numbers and stole the crops and the animals. At last, in their trouble, the Israelites called on God to help them.

God sent a prophet to tell the people that their trouble was because of their disobedience. Then the Angel of the Lord came to Gideon, telling him that he would save Israel from their enemies. The first thing God told Gideon to do, was to break down his father's altar and image. Then he must build an altar and offer a sacrifice to God. Gideon was afraid to do this in the daytime, so he did it at night.

The men of the city were very angry when they saw what had been done. They asked Joash, Gideon's father, to bring Gideon to them, so that they could put him to death. Joash defended his son by saying that if Baal really was a god, he could speak up for himself against Gideon. Joash then gave Gideon the name Jerrubbaal, which means 'let Baal plead'.

God helped Gideon defeat the Midianites and he became the leader, or judge, in Israel. The people then had forty years of peace, but they had not learned their lesson. As soon as Gideon died, they returned to the worship of the false god, Baal. They had been warned many times that while they were faithful to God, He would bless them. However, God would not help them when they bowed down to useless idols.

BiBLE SEARCH:

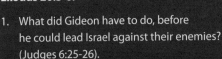

Judges 6:1-16; 25-32; Exodus 19:5-8; Exodus 20:3-6.

1. What did Gideon have to do, before he could lead Israel against their enemies? (Judges 6:25-26).

2. How did Gideon's father defend his son against those who wanted to kill him? (Judges 6:31 – last sentence).

16 NAOMI'S SAD NAME

Ruth 1:20

Naomi lived through some difficult years. Her troubles began with a famine in the land of Israel. Her husband, Elimelech, took her and their two sons into the country of Moab, east of the Dead Sea. However, things did not go well for the family. Elimelech died, leaving Naomi a widow. Both her sons married Moabite women, who would have been brought up to worship idols.

Both of Naomi's sons died, so her family now consisted of three widows. It was extremely difficult in those days for these women, with no man to support them.

Good news reached Naomi: there was now sufficient food in Israel. She decided to make the journey back to her hometown of Bethlehem. Her two daughters-in-law set out with her, but Naomi advised them to return to their own country. Orpah did go back to Moab, but Ruth was determined to stay with Naomi and to worship Naomi's God.

As the two women came to Bethlehem, there was some excitement at seeing Naomi after so many years away. No doubt the years had brought changes to her appearance, so that the women said, 'Is this Naomi?' The name Naomi means 'pleasant', and so she asked them not to call her by that name, but to call her Mara, which means 'bitter'. Naomi felt that God had dealt bitterly with her.

All these events are recorded in the first chapter of the Book of Ruth. The remaining chapters show how Naomi's bitter feeling was completely changed. In time, Ruth married a wealthy relation of Elimelech's named Boaz. The birth of their little son, Obed, was a great joy for Naomi. She could not know that Obed would become the grandfather of King David, from whose family many years later, the Lord Jesus would be born.

BIBLE SEARCH:

Ruth chapter 1 – *(If possible, read the whole book).*

1. What five promises did Ruth make to Naomi? (Ruth 1:16-17).

2. Why did Naomi think that her name should be changed? (Ruth 1:20–21).

17 A PRAYER ANSWERED
1 Samuel 1:20

Hannah was so sad that she could not eat. Her husband Elkanah had two wives as many men did at that time. His other wife, Peninnah, was very unkind to Hannah. She made Hannah's life miserable, by always reminding her that she had children, whilst Hannah had none. The worst time for Hannah was their yearly visit to the tabernacle at Shiloh.

After a meal that she could not eat, Hannah went on her own to the tabernacle. Eli the priest saw her. Unable to stop her tears, Hannah prayed that God would give her a son. She made a promise that if God answered her prayer, she would give that son to Him.

Eli thought Hannah was drunk as he saw her lips moving, but she made no sound. Hannah explained that she was praying out of her great sorrow. The priest then spoke kindly to her, and she returned to her family, no longer sad. Hannah's situation was the same as before, except that she believed that God had heard her prayer.

Hannah did have a son and she named him Samuel, which means 'heard by God'. While Samuel was still a child, Hannah took him to the priest at Shiloh. She reminded Eli of her prayer, saying, 'for this child I prayed.' As she had promised, she left Samuel at Shiloh, to learn how to help Eli in the tabernacle.

Hannah had other children, but each year she made new clothing for Samuel which she took on the family visit to Shiloh. Samuel was faithful to God all his life and he became the last of Israel's 'Judges', the leaders that God set over His people.

BIBLE SEARCH:

1 Samuel chapter 1.

1. What was Hannah's prayer and what was her promise? (verse 11).

2 What changed after Hannah had prayed? (verse 18).

3. How did Hannah keep her promise? (verses 24-28).

The name Ichabod means 'inglorious' and seems a very strange name for a mother to choose for her baby boy. Glory is all about splendour, magnificence and great beauty. Inglorious has the opposite meaning: nothing to admire but rather something to feel ashamed of.

Ichabod's mother was married to Phinehas the priest, who was one of Eli's sons. Eli knew that his two sons did many wrong things, and that God was displeased with them. We read about God's message to Samuel about them in 1 Samuel chapter 3.

Israel's army was defeated in a battle with the Philistines. Hophni and Phinehas, Eli's two sons, brought the Ark of the Covenant into the army camp. Again, Israel was defeated in battle. Hophni and Phinehas were killed and the Ark of the Covenant was captured.

Eli was a very old man. He seated himself at the roadside and waited for news. He was anxious about the Ark being taken to the battlefield. At last, a man came and told him the terrible news. When he heard that the Ark had been captured, he fell from his seat and died.

All this happened just as Phinehas' wife was due to have her baby. News that her husband and her father-in-law were dead, and that the Ark had been taken by the Philistines, was all too much for her. She said, 'The glory has departed from Israel' and named her new baby 'Ichabod' and she too died. So little Ichabod never knew his mother, but his name is a reminder of a very sad time in the nation of Israel. They had not been faithful to God and so He had allowed them to be defeated by their enemies.

BIBLE SEARCH:

A reminder about the Ark
Exodus 25:8-22 *(verse 16 – 'The Testimony': the two stones on which God wrote the Ten Commandments)*; 1 Samuel 4:10-18.

1. Why did God give instructions for the making of the tabernacle (sanctuary)? (Exodus 25:8).

2. What was placed on top of the Ark and what was its purpose? (Exodus 25:21-22).

3. What three pieces of bad news reached Phinehas' wife? (1 Samuel 4:19).

19 A PEACEFUL REIGN
2 Samuel 12:24

The name Solomon means 'peaceful'. Nathan the prophet called his name Jedidiah which means 'beloved of the Lord', but we do not find this name used again.

King David longed to build a temple at Jerusalem where the Ark of the Covenant, the symbol of God's presence, would be kept. It would also be the place where sacrifices would be offered, as God had instructed. However, Nathan told David that God had said it would be his son who would build the temple. David had fought many battles during his reign, and he understood that the temple would be built at a more peaceful time.

David accepted the message that Nathan gave him, and he did everything possible to prepare for the building and to encourage his son Solomon to begin the task. David gave Solomon the plans for the building, as God had given them to him. He also collected many things that he knew would be needed: gold, silver, bronze, iron, wood and precious stones. The leaders of the tribes of Israel also gave generously for the work.

In the fourth year of Solomon's reign, the building began, and it took seven years to complete. He made sure that all was done according to the plans he had been given. There was a wonderful time of thanksgiving when the Ark of the Covenant was brought to the temple. King Solomon gave thanks to God because He had fulfilled His promise, that David's son would build the temple in a time of peace.

Solomon's reign was free from the many battles that his father had fought. God gave Solomon great wisdom, and he became famous for his wisdom and wealth. Sadly, he married heathen women who brought their idolatry to Israel. God was displeased so, after Solomon's death the kingdom was divided, with one king ruling over the north (known as Israel) and another ruling over the south (known as Judah).

BiBLE SEARCH:

1 Chronicles 22:5-19; 2 Chronicles 6:1-21.

1. Why did God not allow David to build the temple? (1 Chronicles 22:7-10).

2. What did Solomon give thanks for? (2 Chronicles 6:4-10).

3. What request did Solomon make? (2 Chronicles 6:19-21).

Kish was one of the captives who had been taken to Babylon from the land of Judah, in the days of Nebuchadnezzar. His family remained in exile when the Babylonian empire fell to the Persians. Mordecai was Kish's great-grandson. He had a cousin whose parents had died. It would seem that he was considerably older than his cousin, because he took care of her.

Mordecai's cousin had been given the Jewish name Hadassah, which means 'myrtle'. However, the name she was known by was Esther, which is probably from the Persian word for star, or from the name of one of the Persian goddesses.

Esther was very beautiful and when the Persian King Ahasuerus was looking for a new wife, Esther was his choice. On her cousin's advice, Esther did not say that she belonged to the Jewish people.

During the time that Esther was the Queen, an evil plan was made to destroy the Jewish people throughout the empire. Mordecai realised how serious this was and that Esther was in a position to plead for her people. God is not named in the Book of Esther, but His ruling over circumstances is clearly seen. Queen Esther did plead for her people, so that they were saved from destruction, and their would-be destroyer was put to death.

God would not allow the nation of Israel to be destroyed, although this was not the only time it was attempted. God had promised that He would send a Saviour into the world. This promised Saviour would be born into the Jewish nation. God is always able to do what He has promised, no matter what circumstances arise. We know that the Lord Jesus Christ was born in the land of Israel. Through His death on the cross, He is the Saviour of all who trust in Him.

BiBLE SEARCH:

Esther 2:6-7; Esther 4 and 5:1-3.

1. What could happen to anyone who tried to see the king without being invited by him? (4:11).

2. What was Mordecai's advice to Esther? (4:12-14).

3. What was King Ahasuerus' response when he saw Esther? (5:2-3).

21 A VERY LONG NAME
Isaiah 8:3

Isaiah was a prophet to the southern kingdom of Judah. God gave him messages for the people during the reigns of four kings: Uzziah, Jotham, Ahaz and Hezekiah. Even his two sons were given names that were a part of what Isaiah was to tell the people.

In the time of King Ahaz, the people of Judah were very troubled. The northern kingdom of Israel had joined with Syria, to make war against Jerusalem. However, God did not allow them to defeat Jerusalem. He instructed Isaiah to name his son Maher-Shalal-Hash-Baz, which means 'speed the spoil, hasten the booty'. Spoil and booty are words for the goods a victorious army takes away from its defeated enemy (we might use the word 'plunder'). God then explained to Isaiah that before his little boy could speak properly, Israel and Syria would be defeated by the King of Assyria.

Ahaz was not a good king. He became an idolater like the kings of the northern kingdom were. It is not surprising that enemies came against Jerusalem during his reign. God would not bless His people while they worshipped useless idols. And yet God was very patient with the people of Judah. There would be a time when Jerusalem would be overcome, and its people taken into captivity but, until that time, God made it clear that He was in control of what happened to Jerusalem. He would not allow its enemies to defeat Judah when they chose.

So we can learn something from a strange name given to a little boy. God is in control of what happens in our world. He may allow, or send, troubled times to nations that have turned away from Him. However, even in times of trouble, He is teaching those who love Him to trust Him more.

BiBLE SEARCH:

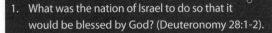

2 Kings 16:1-5; Isaiah 8:1-4;
Deuteronomy 28:1-15 and 25.

1. What was the nation of Israel to do so that it would be blessed by God? (Deuteronomy 28:1-2).

2. What did the people of Judah fear? (2 Kings 16:5).

3. Why did God say they need not fear this? (Isaiah 8:4).

When he was a young man, God called Jeremiah to be a prophet. This would not be easy: Jeremiah would bring messages from God to the people of Judah, that they did not want to hear. The people liked to listen to false prophets who told them that everything would go well. Jeremiah told the people the truth: that God would punish them for their sin.

God was patient with His people, even though they had forgotten all His goodness to them and were worshipping idols. God told Jeremiah to write on a scroll all the messages He had given to him, about what would happen if the people did not change their ways. Jeremiah sent for Baruch, who wrote all the words that God had spoken. At this time, Jeremiah was not allowed to move about freely. He sent Baruch to the temple, to read from the scroll to all the people there.

One man, Michaiah, went to the king's home and told the chief men of Judah who were there, what Baruch had read. They then sent for Baruch to read the scroll to them. They became afraid when they heard what God said, and decided that the king himself must hear. But first Baruch and Jeremiah should go into hiding.

A man named Jehudi read the scroll to the king, while the chief men stood by. The king took a knife and cut the scroll and threw all the pieces in the fire, to burn.

God saw what the king had done. He instructed Jeremiah to rewrite the first scroll. Baruch once again wrote all that Jeremiah told him.

The name Baruch means 'blessed' or 'happy'. However, Baruch was not happy. The king had rejected all that he had faithfully written down. However, God had a message for Baruch. He would be kept safe wherever he went. He was blessed: God remembered him, even when the nation faced death or captivity.

BiBLE SEARCH:

Jeremiah chapters 36 and 45.

1. Why did God ask Jeremiah to write all the words that He had spoken to him? (Jeremiah 36:2-3).

2. What did the king do when the scroll was read to him? (Jeremiah 36:23).

3. What was God's promise to Baruch? (Jeremiah 45:5).

23 A PROPHET IN EXILE

Ezekiel 2:3

Ezekiel was a priest who God called to be a prophet. His name means 'God will strengthen', and he certainly needed to be given strength for his task. He was among the captives taken to Babylon when Nebuchadnezzar conquered Jerusalem. So Ezekiel brought God's message to Israel, at a very sad time in the life of the nation.

God had chosen Israel to be the nation through which the promised Saviour would be born. God had also given His laws to Israel, with the promise of His blessing if they were obedient. They should have shown how good it was to obey God's instructions. Sadly, Israel was disobedient and became idolatrous like the other nations.

God sent prophets, such as Isaiah and Jeremiah, to warn the people of what would happen if they kept worshipping useless idols. God would not bless His people while they bowed down to statues. Those idols had never helped them and never would. The Israelites were clearly told that they would become captives in a foreign land. However, the people preferred to listen to their false prophets, who told them that all would be well.

God warned Ezekiel that just as the people had not listened to the other prophets, so they would not want to listen to him either. However, God said that He had chosen Ezekiel to be a 'watchman' to Israel. A watchman was there to give warning of approaching danger, and so Ezekiel must warn the people that their sin would be punished, if they did not change. God is patient, and so He sends His messengers to sinful people. God is ready to forgive those who repent: those who turn away from their sinful ways (Ezekiel 18:31-32).

BiBLE SEARCH:

Ezekiel 2:1-7; 3:17; Ezekiel 18:20-23; 2 Peter 3:9.

1. What was the difficulty that Ezekiel would face when he brought God's message to the people? (Ezekiel 2:3-7).

2. What gives God no pleasure? What does He want to see? (Ezekiel 18:23).

3. Why does God not always act quickly in punishing people for their evil actions? (2 Peter 3:9).

24 DANIEL'S NEW NAME
Daniel 1:7

Nebuchadnezzar, king of Babylon, besieged the City of Jerusalem, with his army. The king gave instructions that handsome, intelligent young men from good families, should be brought to Babylon to be trained to serve him. They were to be taught the language of Babylon and its literature and knowledge. The training was to last three years and during that time they would have good food and wine, so that they would be strong and healthy to serve the king.

The officer in charge of the young men gave Daniel the name Belteshazzar, a name connected to the Babylonian god Bel. This would have been done with the aim of taking all thought of his own people and his loyalty to God, away from Daniel.

Daniel completed his training and was promoted by Nebuchadnezzar to high office: the king knew that Daniel was both wise and trustworthy. Did the plan to make Daniel forget God and his people succeed? There are many incidents throughout Daniel's life, that show that his love for God was unchanged.

Probably the best-known event of all is recorded in Daniel chapter 6. A law was made to trap Daniel. Some officials who were jealous of Daniel's position, flattered King Darius, by suggesting that for one month no-one should make any request except to him. The punishment for disobedience was to be thrown into the den of lions. Daniel's response was to continue to bring his requests to God. He prayed three times a day, something he had done since he was young.

In many countries today, great pressure is put on Christians to stop being faithful to God. How encouraging to have Daniel's example of standing up to persecution.

BiBLE SEARCH:

Daniel chapter 6.

1. Why were other officials jealous of Daniel? (verse 3).

2. Did Daniel try to hide the fact that he still prayed? (verse 10).

3. What effect did Daniel's safety have on King Darius? (verses 26-27).

25 THREE YOUNG MEN
Daniel 1:7

Like Daniel, Hananiah, Mishael and Azariah were taken to Babylon to be trained to serve the king. They were given names connected with the idols of the Babylonians. They were no longer free men and were expected to give up their loyalty to Israel and Israel's God.

At the end of their three-year training, they were brought before King Nebuchadnezzar. When he talked with them, the King found them wiser than all his magicians and astrologers. He promoted them. Now that they were living in an idolatrous land, would they forget God? The Book of Daniel gives us the answer to this question.

Nebuchadnezzar arranged an elaborate public event for the dedication of a huge golden image about ninety feet high. All the officials were instructed to bow down to the image when music was played. The penalty for disobedience, was to be thrown into the burning fire in a furnace. Not surprisingly, the great crowd was very quick to obey.

A report was brought to the King that three Jewish men, Shadrach, Meshach and Abed-Nego had failed to bow down. The King was furious and demanded that the three men be brought before him. He explained again what was expected of them and gave them a further opportunity to obey. Politely but firmly, they told him that they would not worship the golden image. The record of how God protected the men is found in Daniel chapter 3.

When Shadrach, Meshach and Abed-Nego refused to bow down, they knew that God could save them, but they did not know whether He would choose to do so. Their loyalty to God was not changed by the people's idolatry or the King's threats. The God who kept these three men faithful to Him, is the same God who is able to keep all who trust in the Lord Jesus Christ.

BiBLE SEARCH:

Daniel chapter 3.

1. What is the challenge at the end of verse 15?

2. What happened to the men who threw Shadrach, Meshach and Abed-Nego into the furnace? (verse 22).

3. What effect did the saving of the three men have on Nebuchadnezzar? (verses 28-29).

26 A KING TREMBLES
Daniel 5:23

Bel was the name of one of the chief false gods (idols) of Babylon. King Belshazzar's name meant that Bel protected him.

Belshazzar gave a feast for a thousand of the chief men of Babylon. As they were drinking wine, the king ordered that the beautiful gold and silver drinking vessels from the temple at Jerusalem be brought to the banqueting hall. His guests were to drink wine from them.

In the time of Nebuchadnezzar, many precious things had been brought from the temple at Jerusalem, and then the temple had been burnt down. King Belshazzar thought the false gods of Babylon, were greater than any other nation's gods.

What could have made this proud king tremble, so that he cried out for all his wise men to help him? Suddenly, the feasting and the drinking no longer mattered: the king was afraid. Belshazzar had seen something that terrified him. The fingers of a hand, were writing on the wall of his palace. The king wanted someone to tell him what the writing meant.

Even when he offered great rewards, none of the wise men could understand the writing on the wall. Hearing all that was happening, the queen mother came to the banqueting hall. She remembered Daniel. She told the king about him and he was sent for.

Daniel reminded Belshazzar that Nebuchadnezzar was once a proud king, but God had humbled him. Nebuchadnezzar had then known that Daniel's God was the true and living God. Daniel then explained the writing. The kingdom of Babylon was coming to an end: the Medes and the Persians would take it. Also, God was not satisfied with Belshazzar himself. That same night, Belshazzar was killed and Darius the Mede took over the kingdom.

BIBLE SEARCH:

Daniel 4:28-37; Daniel chapter 5;
Psalm 115:3-8.

1. What was so sinful about what happened at the banquet? (Daniel 5:3-4).

2. What did Belshazzar know about Nebuchadnezzar? (Daniel 4:36-37).

3. What did God say about king Belshazzar? Put this in your own words. (Daniel 5:27).

The name Malachi means 'My messenger', and he was the last of the prophets that God sent to the nation of Israel. However, Malachi wrote about another messenger. One who would prepare people for the coming of God's promised Saviour.

Malachi prophesied about four hundred years before the Lord Jesus was born in Bethlehem. First he told the people what God said about their sin. The priests had become careless about the temple offerings. This showed how little they loved and honoured God. Every sacrifice should have been like a picture of the perfect Saviour who would come. The priests were responsible for teaching about God's law, but they failed to do this.

Malachi also spoke of the sins of the Israelites. They had married people from other nations. God had forbidden this because it would bring idolatry to Israel. Marriage was not upheld as it should have been: divorce was too common. God hates divorce. This is because God's plan for marriage is for a man and woman to be faithful to each other until one of them dies (Genesis 2:24). Malachi's other message was about the Saviour and the one who would prepare for His coming. In the New Testament we read about John the Baptist, the one God had sent to prepare the people for the coming of the Lord Jesus.

Although it was sinful people that God had sent Malachi to, there were also some people who really loved God and were obedient to Him. For these people, God had a special message. We find this in Malachi 3:16-17. This is also an encouragement to Christians today, who live among people who never think about God. You may be the only person in your class at school who is a Christian, but these verses remind us that God knows and remembers you.

BiBLE SEARCH:

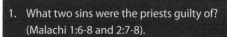

Malachi 1:6-8; 2:7-9; 3:1, 16-17; Mark 1:1-5.

1. What two sins were the priests guilty of? (Malachi 1:6-8 and 2:7-8).

2. Why were the Israelites taught to marry within their own nation? (Malachi 2:11; Deuteronomy 7:1-4).

3. What work would the messenger that Malachi prophesied about, do? (Malachi 3:1).

The name John means 'God is gracious', and so we need to think about what the word 'gracious' means. To be gracious is to show kindness and thoughtfulness to others. When we speak about God being gracious, it means more than this: God is kind to those who do not deserve kindness.

In John's case, his name describes his experience: God was gracious to him. He spent three years with the Lord Jesus, and was also one of the three disciples (Peter, James and John) who were closest to Him. They only were present when Jesus was transfigured, when Jairus' daughter was raised, and they were closest to Him in the Garden of Gethsemane, where Jesus prayed before His crucifixion.

We read that John was the disciple whom Jesus loved. When He was on the cross, the Lord Jesus gave His mother Mary, into John's care. John also had the very special experience recorded in the Book of Revelation. He saw the risen Lord Jesus, who instructed him to write the things he saw. He recorded messages from the Lord Jesus to seven churches, and these messages have much to say to all local churches. He also wrote about the visions he was given, of things that would happen in the world, until the Lord Jesus comes again.

When John wrote his Gospel, he included teaching that Jesus gave to His disciples not found in the other three Gospels (John chapters 14–16).

God was gracious to John and gave him great understanding. God also helped him to write the Gospel, three letters and the Book of Revelation, all of which we have in our New Testament. He had a great desire that others would believe in his Saviour (John 20:30-31) and that they would be sure that they belonged to the Lord Jesus for ever (1 John 5:13).

BiBLE SEARCH:

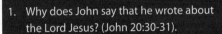

**Mark 1:16-20; John 19:25-27;
John 20:30-31; 1 John 5:11-13.**

1. Why does John say that he wrote about the Lord Jesus? (John 20:30-31).

2. What does John want those who believe in the Lord Jesus to know? (1 John 5:13).

29 A NEW NAME FOR SIMON

John 1:42

Originally Peter was probably named Simeon, a Jewish name, but he used the Greek form, Simon. He was first introduced to the Lord Jesus by his brother Andrew. Jesus gave Simon the name Cephas from the Aramaic word meaning 'a stone'. The New Testament usually uses the Greek word Petros, from which the name Peter comes.

Peter lived near the Sea of Galilee, where he worked as a fisherman. One day while he and Andrew were fishing, Jesus called them to follow Him. They left their fishing nets and went with Jesus, as did two other fishermen, the brothers James and John. Other people also followed the Lord Jesus, but when He chose the twelve disciples, Peter, Andrew, James and John were among them.

For three years Jesus taught His disciples and spoke to great crowds of people. He performed many miracles of healing as well as other miracles such as the feeding of more than five thousand people. Peter was also in a boat with the other disciples when Jesus stilled a great storm on the Sea of Galilee.

When Jesus asked His disciples who they thought He was, it was Peter who replied, 'You are the Christ, the Son of the Living God.' When Jesus spoke of His coming suffering and death, none of the disciples understood.

On the night when the Lord Jesus was arrested and put on trial, Peter denied three times that he even knew Him. It was a frightening time for the disciples: if the Lord Jesus was being so unjustly treated, what might happen to them?

We know that Peter bitterly regretted his denial. We also know that after His resurrection, Jesus again called Peter to follow Him and made it clear that there was work for Peter to do in teaching others.

BiBLE SEARCH:

Matthew 4:18-25; Mark 14:54-72; John 21:15-19.

1. How do we know that the trial of the Lord Jesus was not a fair trial? (Mark 14:56-59).

2. What did Peter deny? (Mark 14:71).

3. How do we know that Peter was forgiven? (John 21:15-19).

30 HELPED BY GOD
John 11:1

Bethany was a village about two miles from Jerusalem. The Lord Jesus was made very welcome at Mary and Martha's home there. One day, the sisters sent a message to Jesus, to tell Him that their brother Lazarus was ill. The Lord Jesus loved this family and yet when He received the message about Lazarus, He did not hurry to Bethany. In fact, He stayed where He was for two more days.

Jesus knew that Lazarus had died from his illness, before He set off for Bethany with His disciples. Mary and Martha both told Jesus that their brother would not have died if He had been there. They believed that Jesus had power to heal, because they knew that He was the Son of God.

When the Lord Jesus came to Lazarus' grave, He asked for the stone to be removed. (A grave in New Testament times, was often a cave with a large stone placed across the entrance.) Martha was surprised that Jesus asked for this to be done, as by this time, Lazarus had been dead for four days. When the stone had been moved, Jesus prayed to His Father and then called with a loud voice, 'Lazarus, come forth!'

Mary and Martha, and the people who had come to comfort them, all saw Lazarus come out of the grave. The Lord Jesus had clearly shown that He even had power over death. The name Lazarus means 'God has helped' and what happened that day was certainly true to his name.

Some of the people who saw that amazing miracle, believed in the Lord Jesus. They knew that only the Son of God could possibly raise the dead. However, others went to tell the Pharisees what they had seen. Instead of giving thanks to God for what had been done, the Pharisees began to plot how they could have Jesus put to death. They hated Him and did not want others to believe in Him.

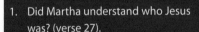

BiBLE SEARCH:

John chapter 11.

1. Did Martha understand who Jesus was? (verse 27).

2. What was it that both sisters said to Jesus? (verses 21 and 32).

3. What effect did this miracle have on the Pharisees? (verse 53).

31 SAUL BECAME PAUL

Acts 13:9

Saul came from Tarsus, in present-day Turkey. He was brought up strictly according to the Jewish law. As an adult, he became a Pharisee, which meant that he was very careful to keep God's commandments and also other laws which had been added to them. As a young man, Saul was present when the first Christian martyr, Stephen, was put to death. He then became very active in persecuting Christians, taking them from their homes so that they could be put in prison.

Saul set out for the city of Damascus to attack the Christians who were there. He intended to bring them to Jerusalem for punishment, but never carried out these plans. On the journey, a light shone around him, and the Lord Jesus spoke to him from heaven. Blinded by the light, he had to be led into Damascus. He now knew that what Christians taught about Jesus, was true. He really had risen from the dead and ascended to heaven.

In Damascus, Saul's sight was restored and he was baptised. Instead of persecuting Christians, he met with them. He then began preaching in the synagogue that Jesus is the Son of God.

Saul became a missionary, travelling through Asia and as far as Europe, bringing the gospel message wherever he went. However, he no longer used his Jewish name, Saul. Instead, he used his Roman name, Paul. This may have been because he knew that God was sending him to the Gentile (non-Jewish) nations.

Paul was called by the Lord Jesus to be an apostle: one sent with a special task to do. Paul wrote at least thirteen of the New Testament letters. We read about his journeys and many things that happened to him, in the Book of Acts.

BiBLE SEARCH:

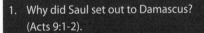

Acts 9:1-31.

1. Why did Saul set out to Damascus? (Acts 9:1-2).

2. In what way was Saul persecuting the Lord Jesus? (Acts 9:4).

3. What became more precious to Paul than all his strict upbringing? (Philippians 3:4-8).

If we learn about some of the things that Joses did, we will understand why he was given the name Barnabas (which means 'Son of Encouragement').

Many people became Christians when they heard the apostles preaching about the Lord Jesus. Some who believed were rich and some were poor. Those who had a lot of possessions sold what they had, so that poor Christians could be helped. The first time we read about Barnabas, is when he sold land and brought the proceeds to the apostles (Acts 4:36-37).

When Saul, who persecuted Christians, became a Christian, his life completely changed. However, the Christians in Jerusalem were afraid of him because they knew how violently he had treated those who believed in the Lord Jesus. They could not believe that Saul the persecutor was now one of them. It was Barnabas who took Saul to the apostles and explained to them that he had already been telling people in Damascus about Jesus. After this, the Christians in Jerusalem accepted Saul.

The Jewish people knew that God had chosen their nation for a special purpose: the promised Saviour would come from this nation. They should have shown other nations how good it was to trust in God and obey His laws. Sadly, they acted as if they were the only people that God cared about. Because of this, some Jewish Christians found it hard to accept that people from other nations (Gentiles) could also become Christians.

News reached the church in Jerusalem that many Greeks in Antioch had believed in the Lord Jesus. Barnabas was sent by the church to Antioch, and he encouraged these new Christians. He then brought Saul from Tarsus and they spent a whole year teaching and helping this new church.

BiBLE SEARCH:

Acts 4:32-37; Acts 9:26-28;
Acts 11:19-26.

1. Why do you think Joses was given the name Barnabas?

2. What practical effect did becoming Christians, have on the rich people? (Acts 4:34).

3. Who did Barnabas bring to help the church in Antioch? (Acts 11:22-25).

33 UNWANTED NAMES

Acts 14:12

The Holy Spirit made it clear to the church in Antioch that they were to send Paul and Barnabas to take the gospel to other countries. So began the first missionary journey to non-Jewish people.

After sailing to Cyprus, Paul and Barnabas visited towns in Asia. In the town of Lystra, Paul spoke to the people about the Lord Jesus. Among those listening was a man who had never been able to walk. Paul told this man to stand up and for the first time in his life, the man stood up and walked.

The people who saw this miracle were amazed and said that the gods had come down to them. Of course, the gods they worshipped were false gods. They called Barnabas, Zeus and they called Paul, Hermes. (These were the names of Greek 'gods', known also by the Roman names of Jupiter and Mercury.)

Paul and Barnabas realised that the people were intending to offer sacrifices to them. As quickly as possible, they ran among the people, telling them that they must not do this, as they were men just like them. They explained that they had come to tell them to stop worshipping false gods, and believe in the true God, who had created the heaven and the earth. It was hard for Paul and Barnabas to persuade the people not to make offerings to them.

What happened next shows us just how changeable people can be. Jews from the towns of Antioch and Iconium arrived. They did not want the people to be taught about Jesus. They stirred up the people to such an extent, that Paul was stoned and dragged out of the city. It appeared at first that Paul had been killed, but he was able to get up. The following day, Paul and Barnabas left Lystra and entered the city of Derbe.

BiBLE SEARCH:

Acts 13:1-4; Acts 14:8-28.

1. Who called Paul and Barnabas to be missionaries? (Acts 13:2).

2. Why did the people of Lystra believe that Paul and Barnabas were gods? (Acts 14:8-11).

3. What was it that made a great change to the way Paul was treated? (Acts 14:19).

34 PAUL'S LOYAL HELPER

2 Timothy 1:1-2

As Paul travelled, taking the gospel message wherever he went, he came to the town of Lystra. There he met a young man named Timothy. The Christians at Lystra spoke well of him. This was Paul's second visit to the town. Timothy probably had become a Christian when Paul had preached the gospel on his first visit. This would explain why Paul called Timothy his son.

The name Timothy means 'honouring God'. To honour someone, means to look up to them with great respect. As we read about him in the New Testament, we find that Timothy lived up to the meaning of his name: he loved and honoured God. This is clear from the way he gave his time and his strength to teaching people about the Lord Jesus. At times he also stayed in a particular place, such as Ephesus, to give further teaching to those who had become Christians.

Paul wrote two letters to encourage and advise Timothy. We have these letters in the New Testament and they are still of great help to us today. They deal with many practical matters about the local churches.

(In the Bible, the word 'church' means people who are Christians: it never means a building.)

Some people think that Timothy may have been a timid or fearful person. We cannot be sure whether this is true, but we do know that Paul encouraged Timothy not to be fearful and to be prepared to face hardship. Being a Christian does not mean that life is going to be easy. Far from it: in the Book of Acts we read about Christians being imprisoned or even put to death. These Christians had not committed any crime but were punished for teaching others about the Lord Jesus. In spite of many difficulties, wherever Paul and his companions went, some people did believe their message and put their trust in the Lord Jesus.

BiBLE SEARCH:

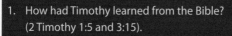

**Acts 16:1-2; 2 Timothy 1:1-8;
2 Timothy 2:1-3; 2 Timothy 3:14-17.**

1. How had Timothy learned from the Bible? (2 Timothy 1:5 and 3:15).

2. What must Timothy not be and what should he be? (2 Timothy 1:7 and 2:3).

3. What must Timothy remember? (2 Timothy 3:14-15).

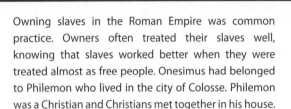

Owning slaves in the Roman Empire was common practice. Owners often treated their slaves well, knowing that slaves worked better when they were treated almost as free people. Onesimus had belonged to Philemon who lived in the city of Colosse. Philemon was a Christian and Christians met together in his house.

Onesimus ran away and may have taken money belonging to Philemon. Somehow, he met the apostle Paul, who was imprisoned, possibly in Rome. Through his meeting with Paul, Onesimus became a Christian. He then showed his gratitude to Paul and his love for the Lord Jesus, by being very helpful to Paul during his imprisonment. Of course, Paul had not committed any crime, but was in prison for preaching the gospel.

Paul wanted to keep Onesimus with him and he thought that Philemon would agree to this. However, he felt that it was right that Onesimus should return to his master. Philemon could then be the one to decide whether he should stay with him or return to Paul.

Paul wrote a letter for Onesimus to give to Philemon and we have this letter in the New Testament. We are not told exactly how Onesimus was received back at Colosse, but we do read about him in Paul's letter to the Christians in Colosse. Here Paul described Onesimus as a 'faithful and beloved brother' (Colossians 4:9).

The name Onesimus means 'useful' or 'profitable', which is why Paul speaks of him as having been unprofitable (running away) but now profitable, as his name describes him.

BiBLE SEARCH:

Philemon; Colossians 4:1-9.

1. Paul called Onesimus his son 'begotten' while in prison. What does he mean by this? (To beget means to give birth to). (Philemon 10 and John 3:3).

2. How did Paul want Philemon to receive Onesimus? (Philemon 15-16).

3. What was Paul's instruction to those who had slaves (bondservants)? (Colossians 4:1).

36 JESUS THE SAVIOUR
Matthew 1:21

The name Jesus means 'Saviour'. Joseph was told by the angel, to give this name to Mary's child. This name tells us that the purpose for which Jesus came into the world was to save. Our Bible verse tells us that it is our sin that we need to be saved from.

In Genesis chapter 3, we read about how sin came into the world, through the disobedience of Adam and Eve. Since that time, everyone born into this world, except the Lord Jesus, has a sinful nature (Romans 3:23). Sin separates us from God, who is perfectly pure and holy. God hates the sin which brings violence and hatred, sorrow and suffering into our lives. God has said that sin results in death (Genesis 2:17 and Romans 6:23). He will not allow sin to enter heaven (Revelation 21:27).

The main world religions teach that people must do things, to be accepted by the 'god' they worship. Only the Bible teaches that we can do nothing to make our peace with God. Only God could do what was needed to bring us into a right relationship with Him.

When the Lord Jesus died on the cross, He took the punishment for the sin of everyone who trusts in

Him. However, He did more than this: He lived a life of perfect obedience to God His Father, something that we could not do. The Bible says that our 'good deeds' are like covering ourselves with dirty rags (Isaiah 64:6). When we trust in the Lord Jesus, God sees us as covered with His purity: like perfectly white clothing in place of dirty rags.

Jesus told the story of two men who went to pray at the temple. The proud Pharisee told God how good he was. The tax collector confessed that he was a sinner: the Lord Jesus said that the tax collector was the one who was justified (put right) with God.

BiBLE SEARCH:

Matthew 1:18-21; Luke 18:9-14; Romans 3:23 and 6:23.

1. Why could only the Lord Jesus give His life as a perfect sacrifice, so that our sin could be forgiven? (Hebrews 7:26-28 – the High Priest is Jesus, the Son of God).

2. What was the main difference between the two men who went to the temple to pray? (Luke 18:9-14).

3. What must we do if our sins are to be forgiven? (1 John 1:9).

The Greek word 'Christ' and the Hebrew word 'Messiah' both mean 'anointed One'. The Jewish people were expecting their Messiah to be an anointed King. They knew that God had promised that King David's descendants would reign for ever. The Messiah that they expected, would make Israel a great Kingdom. The word 'Christ' is not found in the Old Testament and the word 'Messiah' is only used once in the Book of Daniel. Yet, God's promise to send a deliverer, can be found from Genesis to Revelation.

When the Lord Jesus was born in Bethlehem, the wise men travelled to Jerusalem, believing that the 'King of the Jews' had been born. They expected that his birth would be in Israel's capital city. The Bible does not tell us how they knew about this. However, Daniel had lived in Babylon and Persia during the captivity of the Jews, and his prophecies do give an indication of when the Messiah would come (Daniel 9:25).

The religious leaders of the Jews did not accept Jesus as the Messiah, because He did not come in the way they expected. He did not come as the great King who would free them from the Roman Empire. In fact, the Lord Jesus would not allow the people to make Him their King, when they had seen the miracle of the feeding of more than five thousand people (John 6:14-15).

The prophecies of the Old Testament, taught that the One God promised to send, would suffer (Isaiah 53; Daniel 9:26; Psalm 22). After His resurrection we read how Jesus explained these things to Cleopas and his companion, who were travelling to Emmaus (Luke 24:25-27). When the Lord Jesus comes again, as He promised to do, He will then be seen in all His power and glory. Until then, His kingdom is in the hearts of those who love Him.

BiBLE SEARCH:

Isaiah chapter 53; Luke 24:13-27; John 4:25-29.

1. What did Daniel and Isaiah both say would happen to the Messiah? (Daniel 9:26 and Isaiah 53:8)

2. What did the Lord Jesus say that Cleopas and his companion should have known? (Luke 24:25-26).

3. The Lord Jesus told the Samaritan woman that He was the Christ. (John 4:25-26) What had also convinced her that this could be so? (John 4:16-18 and 29).

38 JESUS THE REDEEMER

1 Peter 1:18-19

Redemption means paying a price to rescue someone from a bad situation. In the Old Testament we read of how a poor man's possessions could be redeemed by a relative, and restored to him. A slave could also be redeemed and his freedom purchased by a relation. (Leviticus 25:25-27; 47-49).

The Lord Jesus is the Redeemer of everyone who trusts in Him. He redeems those who belong to Him, from the power and the penalty of sin. The price He paid was His blood shed on the cross. The penalty of sin is death and Jesus died in the place of sinful people who trust in Him.

Those who believed God's promises in the Old Testament days, looked forward to the Redeemer whom God would send. Job trusted in God's promise (Job 19:25-26). King David spoke of God as his Redeemer (Psalm 19:14). At the time of Jesus' birth there were people eagerly expecting the Redeemer (Luke 2:36-38).

Until God's Holy Spirit works in our hearts, we do not realise that we cannot free ourselves from the sin that separates us from God. The Holy Spirit helps us to understand what the Lord Jesus meant when He said, '… whoever commits sin is a slave of sin' (John 8:34). Of course, everyone likes to think that they are free. However, if we try to live up to God's perfect standard, we will find that we cannot do this. We neither love God with all our hearts, nor love others as ourselves (Matthew 22:36-40). We need to know the Lord Jesus as our Redeemer, who not only forgives our sin, but also sends His Holy Spirit to help us to live in a way that pleases God.

BiBLE SEARCH:

Leviticus 25:25-27 and 47-49;
Job 19:25-26; Ruth 4:1-10.

1. Who could redeem property that had been sold, or redeem someone from slavery? (Leviticus 25:25-27 and 47-49).

2. Who was willing to act as a redeeming relative in the Book of Ruth? (Ruth 4:9).

3. What payment was made so that we could be redeemed and who paid that price? (1 Peter 1:18-19).

39 THE PRINCE OF PEACE

Isaiah 9:6

Another name given to the promised Saviour is 'Prince of Peace'. Sadly, it is because this world does not know the Prince of Peace, that it has so often been filled with war and violence. When angels brought news of the Saviour's birth to the shepherds, they said, 'Glory to God in the highest, and on earth peace …' (Luke 2:14). We might ask, has there really been peace on earth since He came? There will certainly be peace when Jesus comes again, but where is that peace now?

The Lord Jesus gives peace with God, to everyone who trusts in Him. Left to ourselves, we do not want God. We are enemies of God (Colossians 1:20-21) and we want to go our own way. Because God is our Creator who knows what is best for us, going our own way through life, brings all sorts of trouble. Being reconciled to God, means knowing God as our loving Heavenly Father. We can only be reconciled to God, when we trust in the Lord Jesus to forgive the sin that separates us from God.

The Lord Jesus also gives peace between those who belong to Him. Whatever nationality, whatever skin colour, rich or poor: there is peace between those who trust in the same Saviour (Galatians 3:28). If we are Christians, we know that all are equal before God: we are all sinners who have been forgiven through faith in Christ.

It is very easy to become troubled and anxious about the future. The Bible contains many promises of peace to those who are trusting in God. Whether we are concerned about our own future, or about things which are happening in the world around us, we will be wise to commit some of these promises to memory.

BiBLE SEARCH:

Some promises to learn. Isaiah 26:3; John 14:27; Philippians 4:6-7.

1. Who will be kept in perfect peace? (Isaiah 26:3).

2. Why should we not be troubled or afraid? (John 14:27).

3. What should we do instead of becoming anxious? (Philippians 4:6).

The promise of a Saviour is found first in Genesis 3, after Adam and Eve sinned. That promise continued right through the Old Testament. So, how was sin to be dealt with until Jesus came? How could people in the Old Testament days find forgiveness? God had said that sin would bring death (Genesis 2:17), but He provided a way so that the sinner could be forgiven.

In the book of Exodus we read God's instructions for the tabernacle (a special tent), where priests would offer sacrifices. An animal had to die, in place of the person who had sinned. Of course no animal could take sin away, but every sacrifice was like a picture of what the promised Saviour would do. As they offered their sacrifices, the people were trusting in what God had promised.

Moses' brother Aaron was the first High Priest and his sons were priests. There were certain tasks in the tabernacle, that only the High Priest could do. Only he could enter the Most Holy Place, the room in the tabernacle where the sign of God's presence called the Ark of the Covenant was. Even the High Priest could enter there just once a year on the Day of Atonement.

The Book of Hebrews describes the Lord Jesus as our Great High Priest. The Old Testament priests had to offer sacrifices for their own sin as well as for the people's sin. The Lord Jesus is completely without sin, and He offered Himself as a perfect, never-to-be-repeated sacrifice. God accepted Christ's sacrifice as being sufficient for every man, woman, boy or girl, who trusts in Him.

God is perfectly pure and holy. He hates sin: the selfishness, envy, hatred and violence. He will punish sin unless we seek His forgiveness. When God's Holy Spirit works in our hearts, we feel our own sinfulness. We know that we have broken God's laws. The Bible teaches us that we cannot put this right, but the Lord Jesus has done everything that we cannot do.

BiBLE SEARCH:

John 3:16; Acts 16:31; 1 John 1:7-9; Hebrews 9:11-14 and 24-28.

1. What was the sacrifice that the Lord Jesus offered? (Hebrews 9:14).

2. Are any further sacrifices needed? (Hebrews 9:28).

3. How do we find forgiveness? (1 John 1:9).

Good Choices, Bad Choices
by Jean Stapleton

The Bible teaches us that God always does what He says He will do. It is a great comfort to know, that God's plans and purposes are not changed by men and women who make wrong or foolish choices. In a way that we cannot understand, God rules over everything, so that His promises are always fulfilled. From the first wrong choice made by Adam and Eve throughout the Bible we meet many people who chose well or who made foolish decisions. This book will help you to focus on God's Word and his wisdom guiding you in your own day to day choices.

ISBN: 978-1-5271-0527-0

More Good Choices, Bad Choices
by Jean Stapleton

The Bible teaches us that God always does what He says He will do. It is a great comfort to know, that God's plans and purposes are not changed by men and women who make wrong or foolish choices. In a way that we cannot understand, God rules over everything, so that His promises are always fulfilled. Young and old, rich and poor all appear in the Bible and through them we see examples of people who made wise and foolish decisions. This book will help you to focus on God's Word and his wisdom guiding you in your own day to day choices.

ISBN: 978-1-5271-0528-7

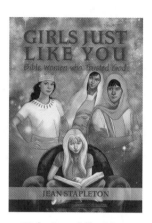

Girls Just Like You
by Jean Stapleton

We might think that people in Bible times were different from us (much braver and better than we are), but that isn't true. They were just like us – just like you, in fact! There are fifty different stories in this book, with Bible verses to read that will teach you about the girls and women in the Bible who trusted God. Find out about them and about yourself by discovering God's Word that He has written for you!

ISBN: 978-1-78191-997-2

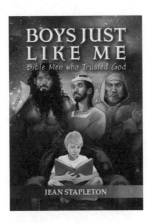

Boys Just Like Me
by Jean Stapleton

We might think that people in Bible times were different from us (much braver and better than we are), but that isn't true. They were just like us – just like you, in fact! There are fifty different stories in this book, with Bible verses to read that will teach you about the boys and men in the Bible who trusted God. Find out about them and about yourself by discovering God's Word that He has written for you!

ISBN: 978-1-78191-998-9

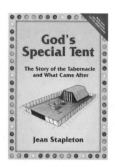

God's Special Tent
by Jean Stapleton

Do you like tents? Perhaps you've gone camping, staying in one place and then moving to another. God's people the Israelites lived in tents in the wilderness as they moved from Egypt to the Promised Land. God gave them instructions about how to make a special tent – where He could be present among His people. The priests made sacrifices to atone for the sin of the people, but the tabernacle or tent of meeting was a place that taught the people about the one who was going to save them from their sin for good - Jesus Christ, the promised Messiah. His sacrifice would mean that no other sacrifices were needed and that people could worship God all around the world.

ISBN: 978-1-84550-811-1

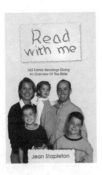

Read with me
by Jean Stapleton

Read with Me takes the stories and teachings of the Bible from the beginning of the Old Testament through to the end of the New, explaining them in simple, direct language. These devotions are ideal for reading to children – each one bringing out truths and questions, answers and lessons – and will bring your family closer to God.

For older family members there is also an additional feature where, throughout the book, introductions are given to those Old and New Testament books that are featured. These give useful information for older children – or for adults to read alongside the family devotions.

ISBN: 978-1-84550-148-8

Christian Focus Publications publishes books for adults and children under its four main imprints: Christian Focus, CF4K, Mentor and Christian Heritage. Our books reflect our conviction that God's Word is reliable and Jesus is the way to know him, and live for ever with him.

Our children's publication list covers pre-school to early teens. We also publish personal and family devotional titles, biographies and inspirational stories that children will love.

From pre-school board books to teenage apologetics, we have it covered!

Christian Focus Publications Ltd,
Geanies House, Fearn, Ross-shire,
IV20 1TW, Scotland,
United Kingdom.
www.christianfocus.com